THE USBORNE
BIG BOOK OF BIG
STARS
AND PLANETS

Written by Emily Bone

Illustrated by Fabiano Fiorin

Designed by Stephen Wright
Space expert: Stuart Atkinson

Series designer: Josephine Thompson Series editor: Jane Chisholm
Additional design by Will Dawes and Vickie Robinson
Image manipulation by Nick Wakeford and John Russell

Our planet

We live on Planet Earth, a huge,
round lump of rock floating in space.

A layer of gases – called the
atmosphere – gives us **air** to
breathe, and makes sure we
don't get too hot or too cold.

The white swirls
are **clouds**. Rain falls
from the clouds, which
makes plants grow.

Earth is a very wet planet.
Huge **seas** and **oceans** cover
almost **three-quarters** of
the Earth's surface.

The green and
brown shapes
are **land**.

There are thousands of human-made things in space. **Satellites** are **spacecraft** that fly around the Earth to gather and send information.

The Moon is a rocky ball that travels around the Earth. We can see the Moon in our night sky.

Weather satellites help forecast the weather.

Global Positioning System (GPS) satellites create maps and send directions to our phones, computers and vehicles.

The light patches are mountain ranges on the Moon's surface.

Television satellites send television signals across the world.

These are **meteors** – tiny space rocks that burn up in the Earth's atmosphere.

Over **eight billion people** live on Earth. The lights from big **cities** can be seen from space.

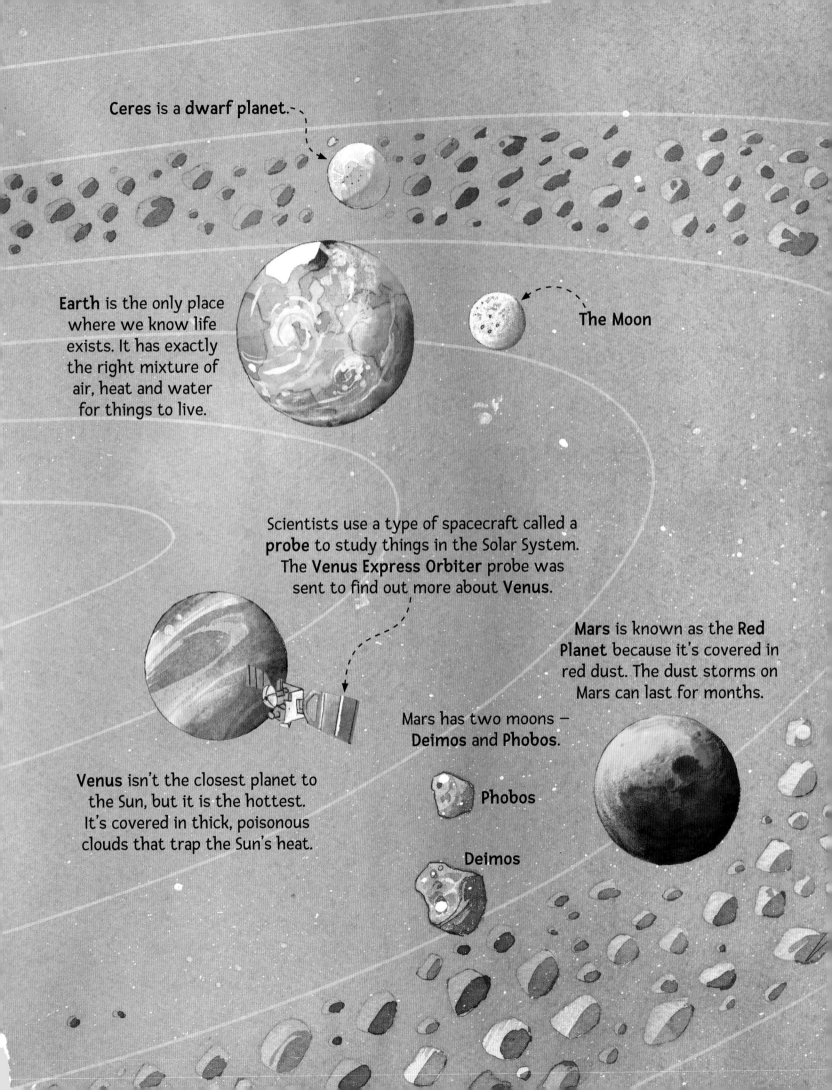

Ceres is a **dwarf planet.**

Earth is the only place where we know life exists. It has exactly the right mixture of air, heat and water for things to live.

The Moon

Scientists use a type of spacecraft called a **probe** to study things in the Solar System. The **Venus Express Orbiter** probe was sent to find out more about **Venus.**

Mars is known as the **Red Planet** because it's covered in red dust. The dust storms on Mars can last for months.

Mars has two moons – **Deimos** and **Phobos.**

Venus isn't the closest planet to the Sun, but it is the hottest. It's covered in thick, poisonous clouds that trap the Sun's heat.

Phobos

Deimos

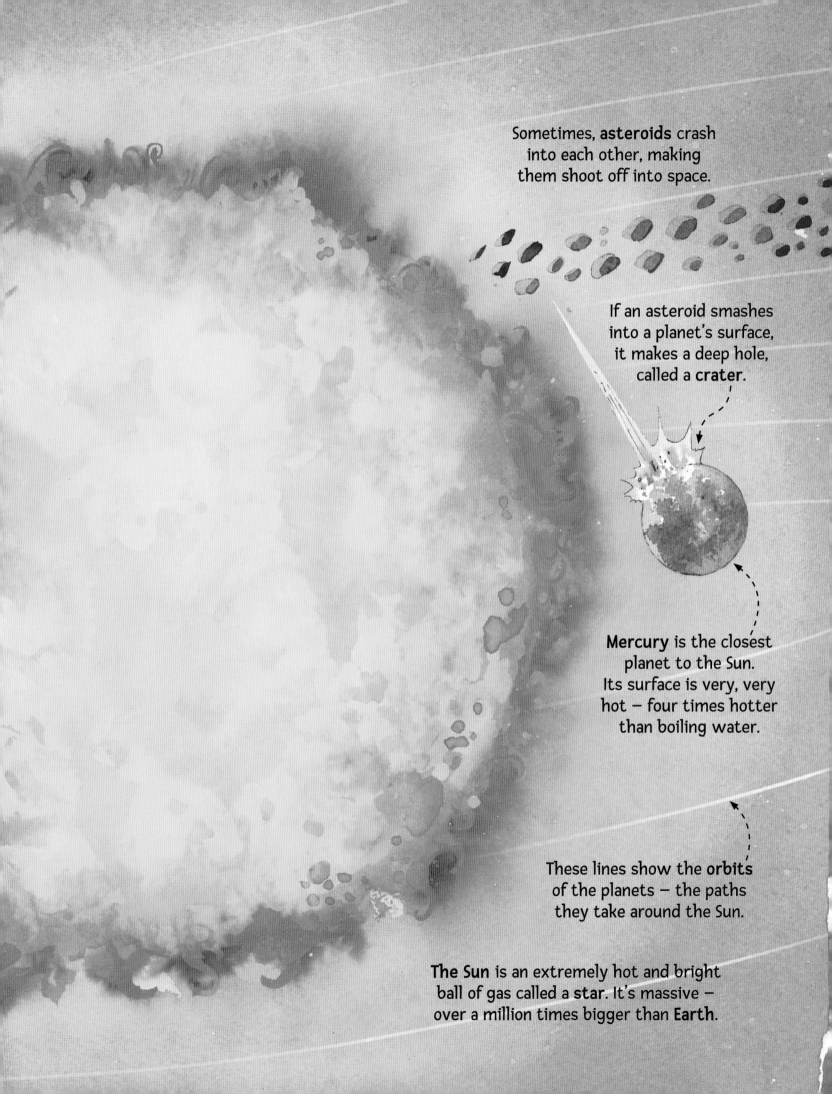

Sometimes, **asteroids** crash
into each other, making
them shoot off into space.

If an asteroid smashes
into a planet's surface,
it makes a deep hole,
called a **crater**.

Mercury is the closest
planet to the Sun.
Its surface is very, very
hot – four times hotter
than boiling water.

These lines show the **orbits**
of the planets – the paths
they take around the Sun.

The Sun is an extremely hot and bright
ball of gas called a **star**. It's massive –
over a million times bigger than **Earth**.

The Sun

The Solar System

The Earth is one of eight planets that move around a star called the Sun. The Sun and its planets are known as the Solar System.

A planet's **year** is the time it takes to go once around the Sun. Earth's year is 365 days.

As well as moving around the Sun, planets spin, too. A **day** is the time it takes for a planet to spin around once. Earth's day is just under 24 hours.

Mercury
Year: 88 Earth days
Day: 59 Earth days
Moons: 0

Venus
Year: 225 Earth days
Day: 117 Earth days
Moons: 0

Moons are rocky or icy lumps that travel around some planets.

Mars
Year: 687 Earth days
Day: 24 hours, 30 minutes
Moons: 2

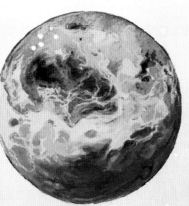

Earth
Year: 365 Earth days
Day: 23 hours, 56 minutes
Moons: 1

All the planets on this page are mostly made of **rock**.

Ida

Eros

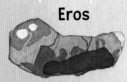

Asteroids are lumps of rock, metal or ice that move around in a big group called the **Asteroid Belt**. Most of the biggest ones have names.

The planets on this page are mostly made of **gas**.

Jupiter
Year: 12 Earth years
Day: 9 hours, 56 minutes
Moons: at least 95

Jupiter is **the biggest planet** in the Solar System.

Saturn
Year: 29.5 Earth years
Day: 10 hours, 42 minutes
Moons: at least 146

Gas planets have **rings** of dust, rock and ice circling them.

Saturn's rings are especially wide and impressive.

Uranus
Year: 84 Earth years
Day: 17 hours, 14 minutes
Moons: at least 28

Neptune
Year: 165 Earth years
Day: 16 hours, 6 minutes
Moons: at least 16

Dwarf planets are larger than asteroids, but smaller than planets. This is the dwarf planet **Pluto**.

The planets are actually very different sizes. Here you can see how big they are compared to each other.

Mercury   Venus   Earth   Mars   **Jupiter**   **Saturn**   Uranus   Neptune

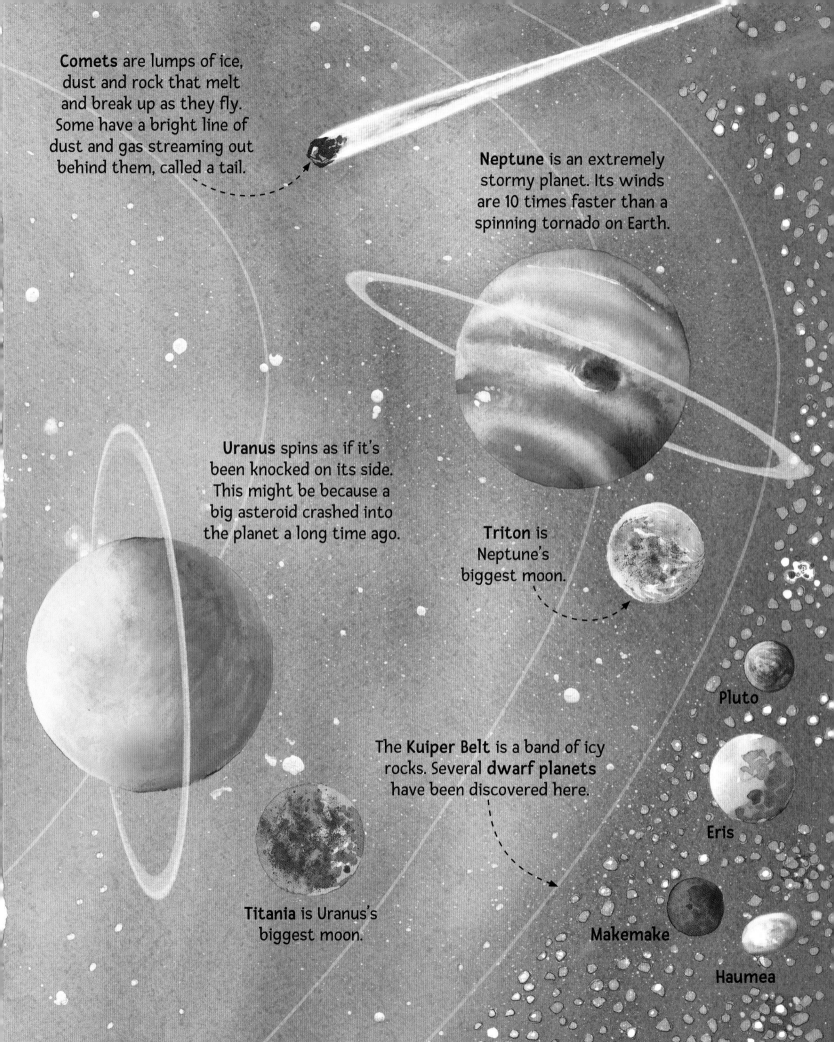

Comets are lumps of ice, dust and rock that melt and break up as they fly. Some have a bright line of dust and gas streaming out behind them, called a tail.

Neptune is an extremely stormy planet. Its winds are 10 times faster than a spinning tornado on Earth.

Uranus spins as if it's been knocked on its side. This might be because a big asteroid crashed into the planet a long time ago.

Triton is Neptune's biggest moon.

The **Kuiper Belt** is a band of icy rocks. Several **dwarf planets** have been discovered here.

Titania is Uranus's biggest moon.

Pluto

Eris

Makemake

Haumea

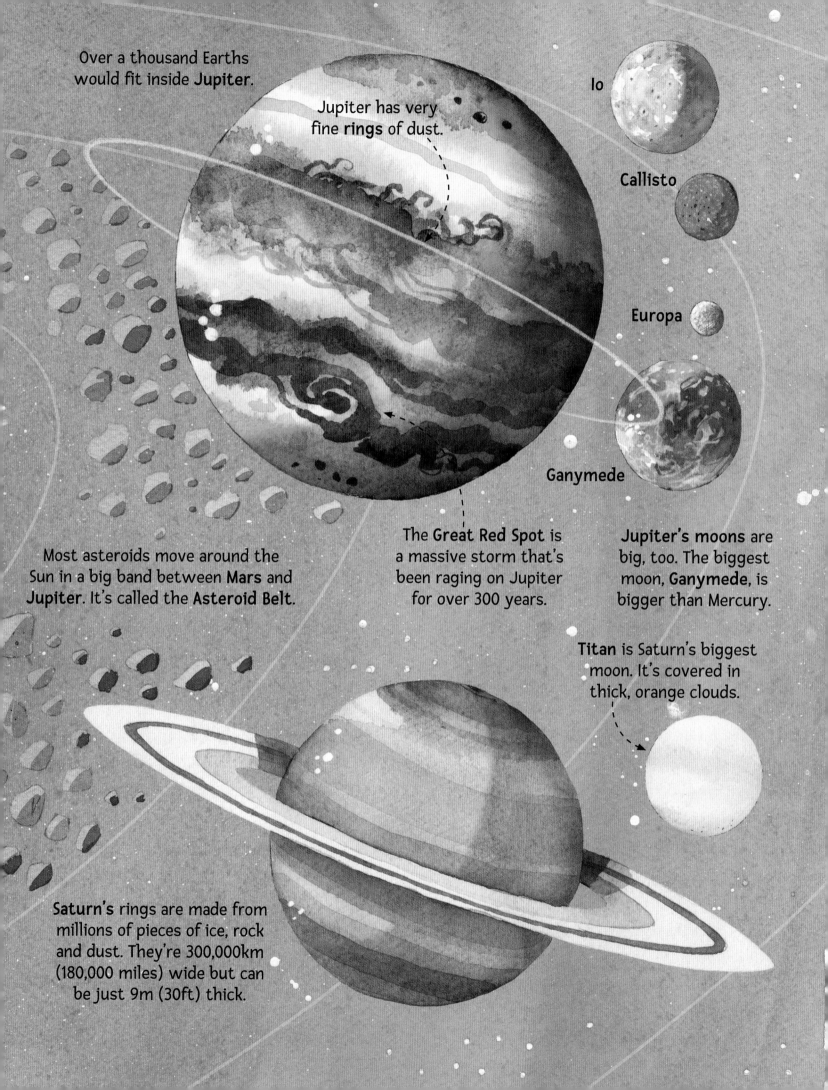

Over a thousand Earths would fit inside **Jupiter**.

Jupiter has very fine **rings** of dust.

Io

Callisto

Europa

Ganymede

Most asteroids move around the Sun in a big band between **Mars** and **Jupiter**. It's called the **Asteroid Belt**.

The **Great Red Spot** is a massive storm that's been raging on Jupiter for over 300 years.

Jupiter's moons are big, too. The biggest moon, **Ganymede**, is bigger than Mercury.

Titan is Saturn's biggest moon. It's covered in thick, orange clouds.

Saturn's rings are made from millions of pieces of ice, rock and dust. They're 300,000km (180,000 miles) wide but can be just 9m (30ft) thick.

The Sun

The Sun is a star – a massive ball of powerful, exploding gases. It gives the planets all their light and heat.

The surface of the Sun bubbles and churns. It's called the **chromosphere** and is 60 times hotter than boiling water.

Solar prominences are huge, fiery loops of gas that shoot out into space. They can be 20 times bigger than the Earth.

Solar tornadoes are fast, whirling funnels of gas. They're thousands of times bigger than tornadoes on Earth.

The **corona** is a layer of hot gases that surrounds the Sun. It's 5,000 times hotter than the surface below.

The Sun lets out a powerful stream of hot gases into space. This is called the **solar wind**.

A **fast riser** is a small, straight jet of gas that flies out of the Sun.

Super stars

There are billions and billions of stars in space.
New stars explode into life from hot, swirling
clouds of gas and dust, called *nebulae*.

Nebulae can create amazing shapes.
This is part of the **Eagle Nebula**.
The dust and gas get very, very hot and
eventually fuse together to become
exploding balls of gas, called **stars**.

Points of light, like
this, are bright
young stars.

The outer layers of some dying stars puff away in clouds of gas. This is the **Cat's Eye Nebula** around a dying star.

The original star has turned into a small, heavy type of star called a **white dwarf**.

Gigantic galaxies

Galaxies are enormous groups
of billions of stars, *nebulae*,
gas and dust. They form
spectacular shapes.

This is an **irregular galaxy** called the **Cartwheel Galaxy**. It was made when two galaxies crashed into each other millions of years ago.

Spiral galaxies have arms that curve out of a bulging, bright middle. This is the **M74 Gemini** galaxy.

Elliptical galaxies are balls of old stars. This one is called **Messier 60**. It was named by Charles Messier, an 18th century astronomer.

There are different types of stars.

After millions and millions of years, a star's gas supply runs out and it starts to die.

Red dwarfs are the smallest and least powerful stars.

Yellow dwarfs produce a steady amount of light and heat. Our **Sun** is a yellow dwarf.

Sometimes, smaller stars circle bigger ones. These are called **binary stars**.

Blue supergiants are huge stars, thousands of times hotter and brighter than the Sun.

A huge star, such as a blue supergiant, ends its life in a massive explosion, called a *supernova*. This one is known as the **Crab Supernova** because it looks a little like a crab's shell.

This is the **Orion Nebula**.
It's one of the closest
nebulae to Earth.

Stars usually form
in **star clusters**.

Some galaxies are **merging**, which means they're slowly joining together to become one huge galaxy.

These are actually two **merging galaxies** called the **Mice Galaxies** because they look a little like mice with long tails.

We're part of the **Milky Way** galaxy, a **barred spiral galaxy** with arms coming out of a bar-shaped middle. Our Sun is just one of its stars.

This is the **Sombrero Galaxy**, named because it looks like a Mexican hat.

Exploring space

Powerful rockets, spacecraft and telescopes help us find out about stars and planets.

The first spacecraft was *Sputnik 1*, a Russian satellite launched in 1957. It flew around the Earth.

From 1969 to 1972, the US *Apollo* missions took astronauts to **the Moon**. The **Command Service Module (CSM)** spacecraft flew them there.

Probes use cameras and other instruments to study planets, moons and other things in space. The *Cassini* probe was launched in 1997.

Space telescopes orbit the Earth. They make things that are very far away look a lot bigger and clearer.

Astronauts wear protective spacesuits.

The **lunar module** separated from the CSM, and flew astronauts to the Moon's surface.

This is the **Hubble Space Telescope**. It was launched in 1990.

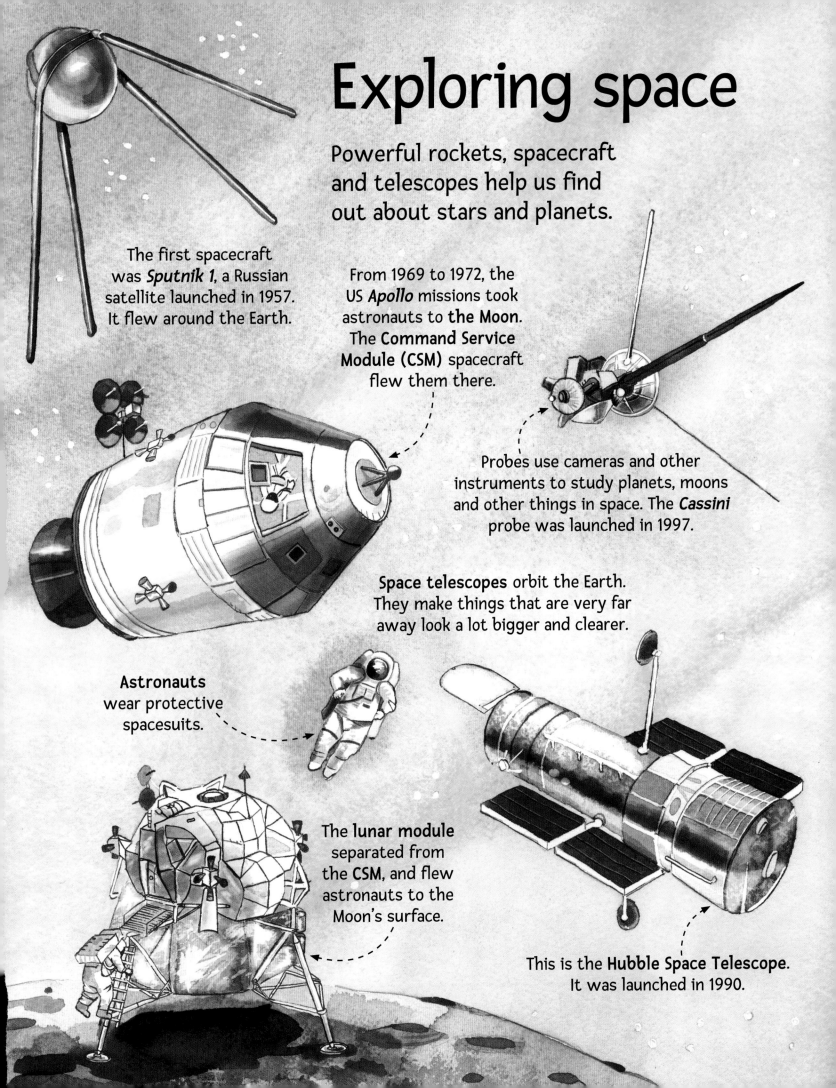

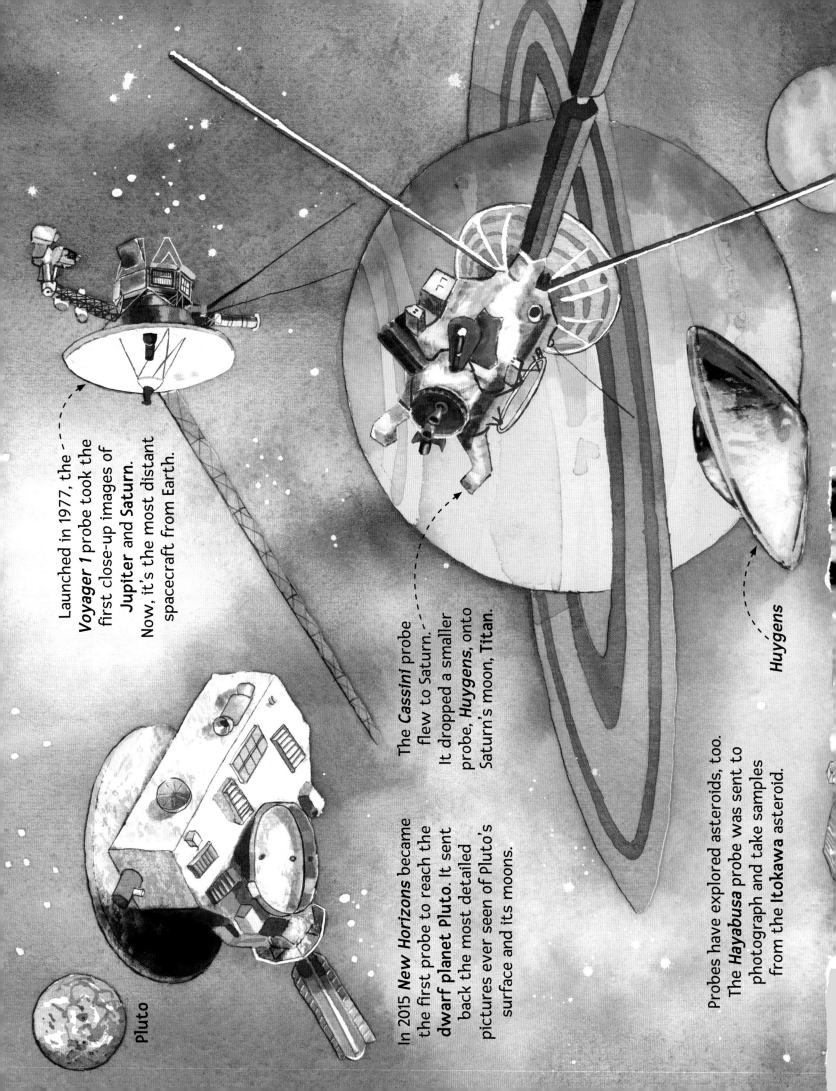

Launched in 1977, the **Voyager 1** probe took the first close-up images of **Jupiter** and **Saturn**. Now, it's the most distant spacecraft from Earth.

The **Cassini** probe flew to Saturn. It dropped a smaller probe, **Huygens**, onto Saturn's moon, Titan.

In 2015 **New Horizons** became the first probe to reach the **dwarf planet Pluto**. It sent back the most detailed pictures ever seen of Pluto's surface and its moons.

Probes have explored asteroids, too. The **Hayabusa** probe was sent to photograph and take samples from the Itokawa asteroid.

Pluto

Huygens

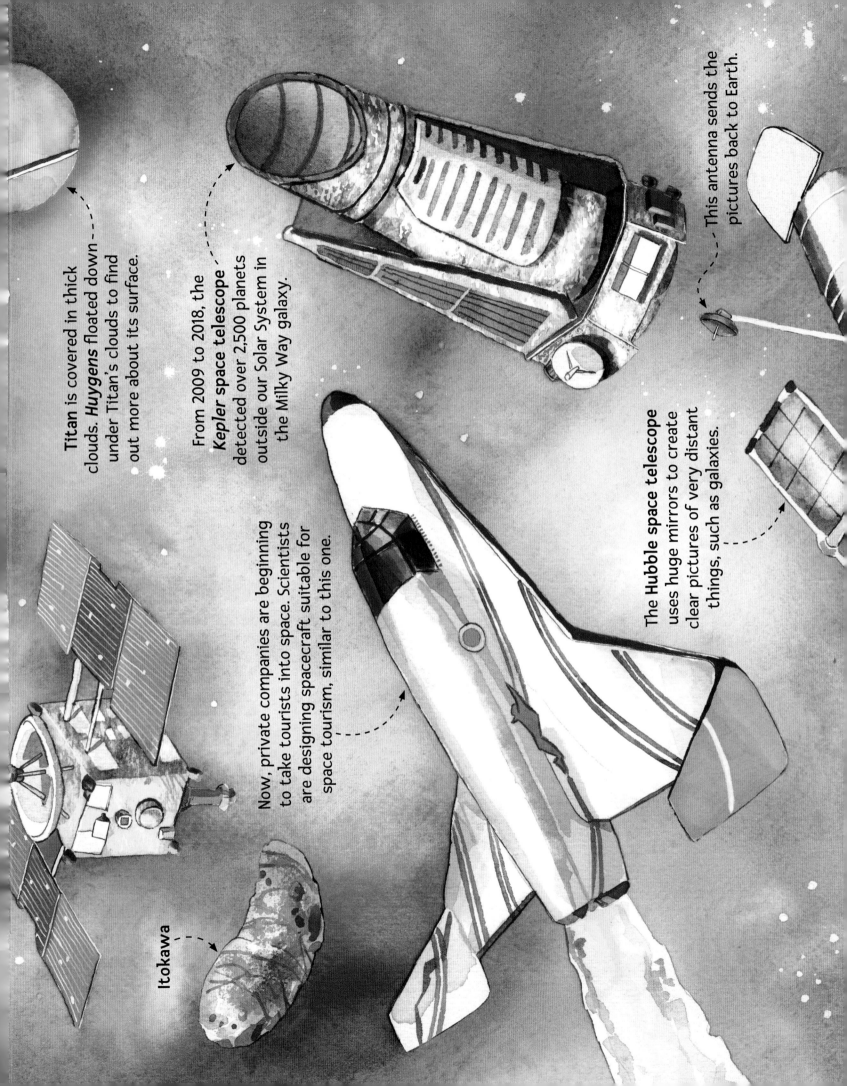

Titan is covered in thick clouds. *Huygens* floated down under Titan's clouds to find out more about its surface.

From 2009 to 2018, the *Kepler* space telescope detected over 2,500 planets outside our Solar System in the Milky Way galaxy.

This antenna sends the pictures back to Earth.

The **Hubble** space telescope uses huge mirrors to create clear pictures of very distant things, such as galaxies.

Now, private companies are beginning to take tourists into space. Scientists are designing spacecraft suitable for space tourism, similar to this one.

Itokawa

The middle of the Milky Way looks very bright because there are lots of hot, glowing stars here.

Galaxies exist together in groups. The Milky Way's group is called the **Local Group**. It has over 30 galaxies in it.

Our **Solar System** is on one of the outer arms of the Milky Way.

The closest galaxy to the Milky Way is the Andromeda Galaxy

The Moon looks as if it's shining, but it isn't. It's sunlight reflecting off the Moon's surface.

Jupiter

You might see the **ISS** crossing the sky. It looks like a bright, moving star.

As the Moon moves around the Earth, the Sun lights up different parts of it.

The other part is in shadow, so it looks dark.

When the **solar wind** hits the Earth's **atmosphere**, it sometimes creates a beautiful light show called an *aurora*.

This misty stripe is what the brightest part of the **Milky Way** galaxy looks like from Earth.

Some planets in the night sky look like bright stars. **Venus** can often be seen close to the horizon.

Usborne Quicklinks

To find out more about stars and planets with videos and activities, scan the QR code or go to **usborne.com/Quicklinks** and type in the title of the book.

Usborne Publishing is not responsible for the content of external websites. Children should be supervised online. Please follow the online safety guidelines at **usborne.com/Quicklinks**

This edition first published in 2024 by Usborne Publishing Limited, 83-85 Saffron Hill, London EC1N 8RT, United Kingdom. usborne.com
Copyright © 2024, 2017, 2010 Usborne Publishing Limited. The name Usborne and the Balloon logo are registered trade marks of Usborne Publishing Limited. All rights reserved. No part of this publication may be reproduced, stored in a retrieval system or transmitted in any form or by any means without prior permission of the publisher. First published in America 2010. This edition first published 2024. UE.

The night sky

If you look up at the sky on a clear night, you can see lots and lots of stars, and many other things, too.

The brightest stars can be grouped into imaginary pictures, called **constellations**. There are 88 in total.

Sirius, or the **Dog Star**, is the brightest star in the night sky.

This is the **Canis Major**, or **Great Dog**, constellation.

One of the most famous constellations is **Orion the Hunter**, named after a hero in Greek mythology.

The bright lights of **Orion's sword** are actually the **Orion Nebula**.

The star **Polaris** always points north.

This is the **Crux**, or **Southern Cross** constellation.

The **Big Dipper** is also known as the **Plough**.

You'll see different things depending on where you are on the Earth. Check online to find out what you can see in your area.

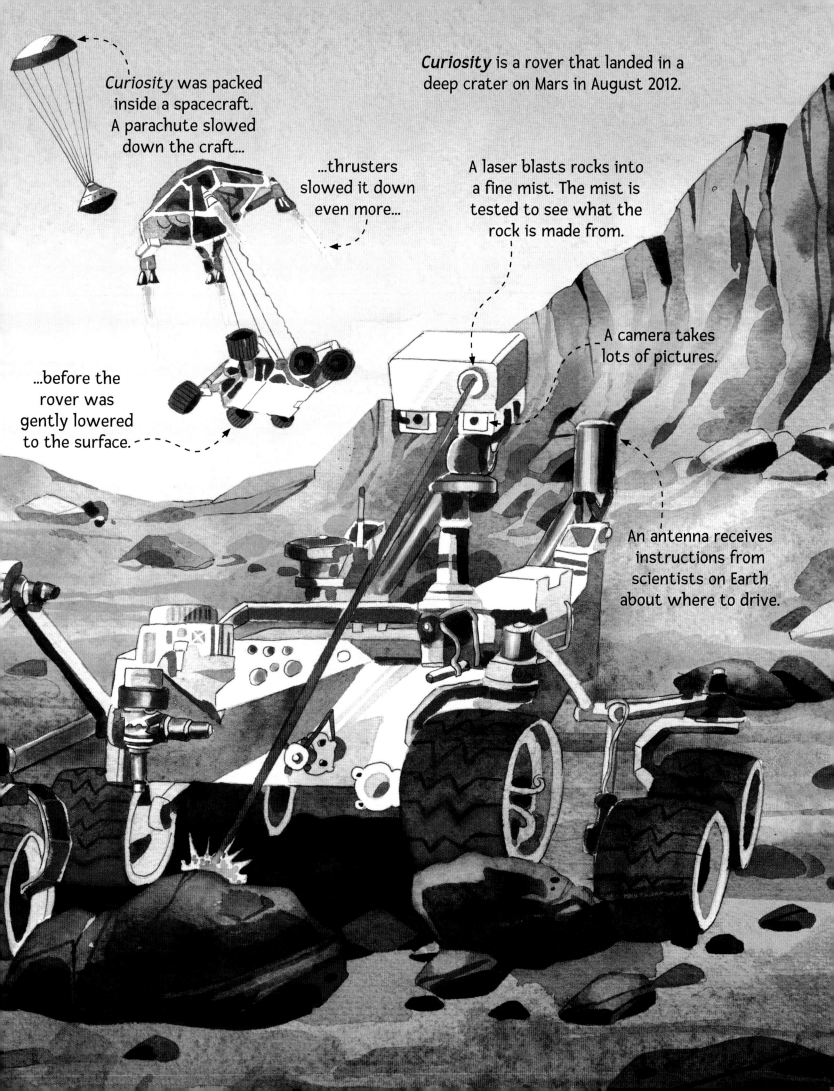

Roving around

The surface of Mars is cold, dusty and dry. But, scientists think that there was water there once, and maybe even life. They've sent robots to Mars to find out more...

Landers stay in one position to take pictures and do experiments. In 1976, the *Viking 1* lander was the first spacecraft to land safely on Mars.

Rovers are vehicles that drive around Mars. They're controlled by scientists on Earth. This rover is called *Opportunity*.

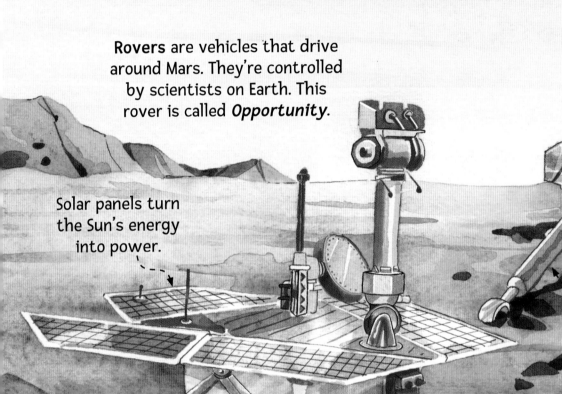

Solar panels turn the Sun's energy into power.

This robot arm collected rock samples.

Opportunity landed on Mars in 2004. It drove to different rocks and examined them to find out if they were ever covered by water or ice. In 2018, it shut down after being caught in a dust storm.

Curiosity drills into rock, then scoops up leftover dust to test it for signs of water.

Drill holes

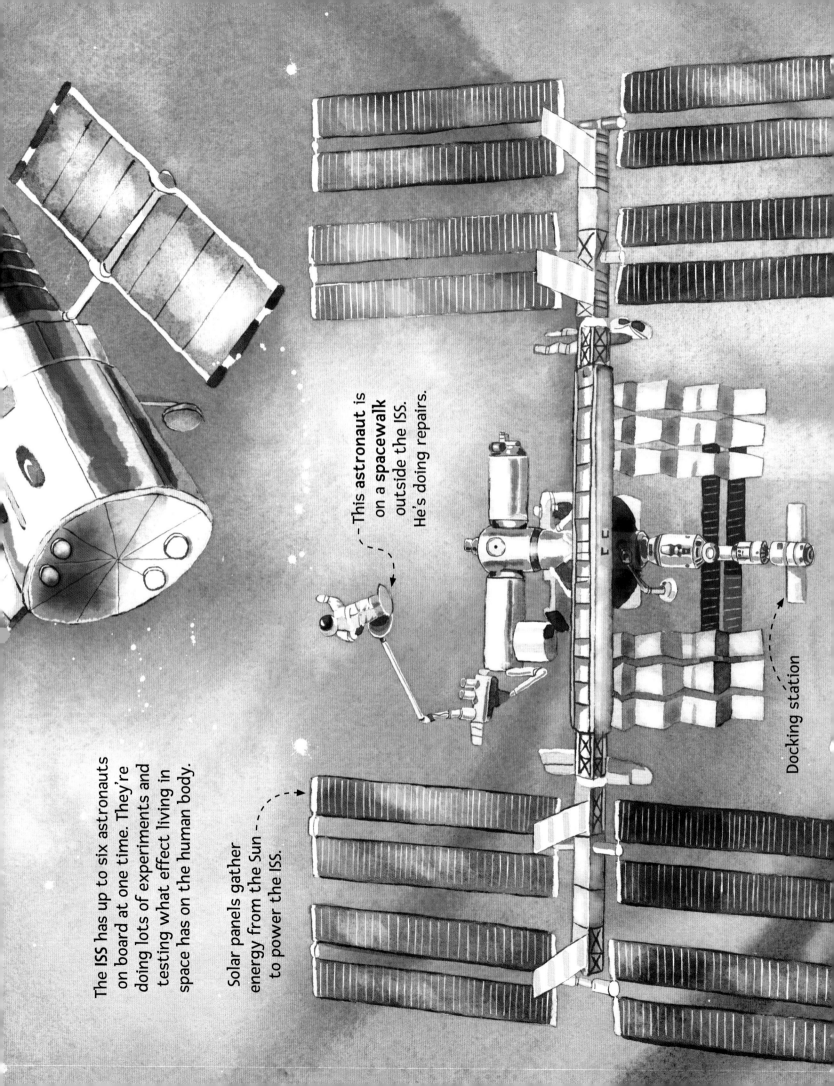

The ISS has up to six astronauts on board at one time. They're doing lots of experiments and testing what effect living in space has on the human body.

Solar panels gather energy from the Sun to power the ISS.

This astronaut is on a spacewalk outside the ISS. He's doing repairs.

Docking station

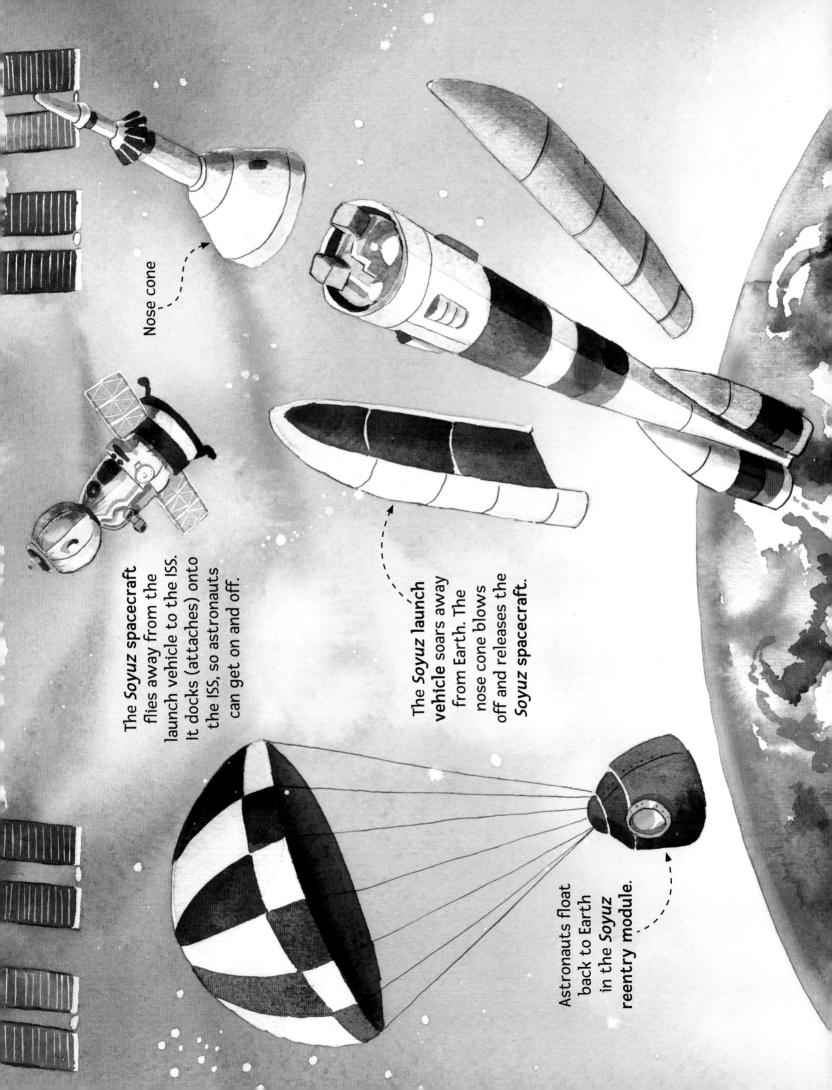

Nose cone

The *Soyuz* spacecraft flies away from the launch vehicle to the ISS. It docks (attaches) onto the ISS, so astronauts can get on and off.

The *Soyuz* launch vehicle soars away from Earth. The nose cone blows off and releases the *Soyuz* spacecraft.

Astronauts float back to Earth in the *Soyuz* reentry module.

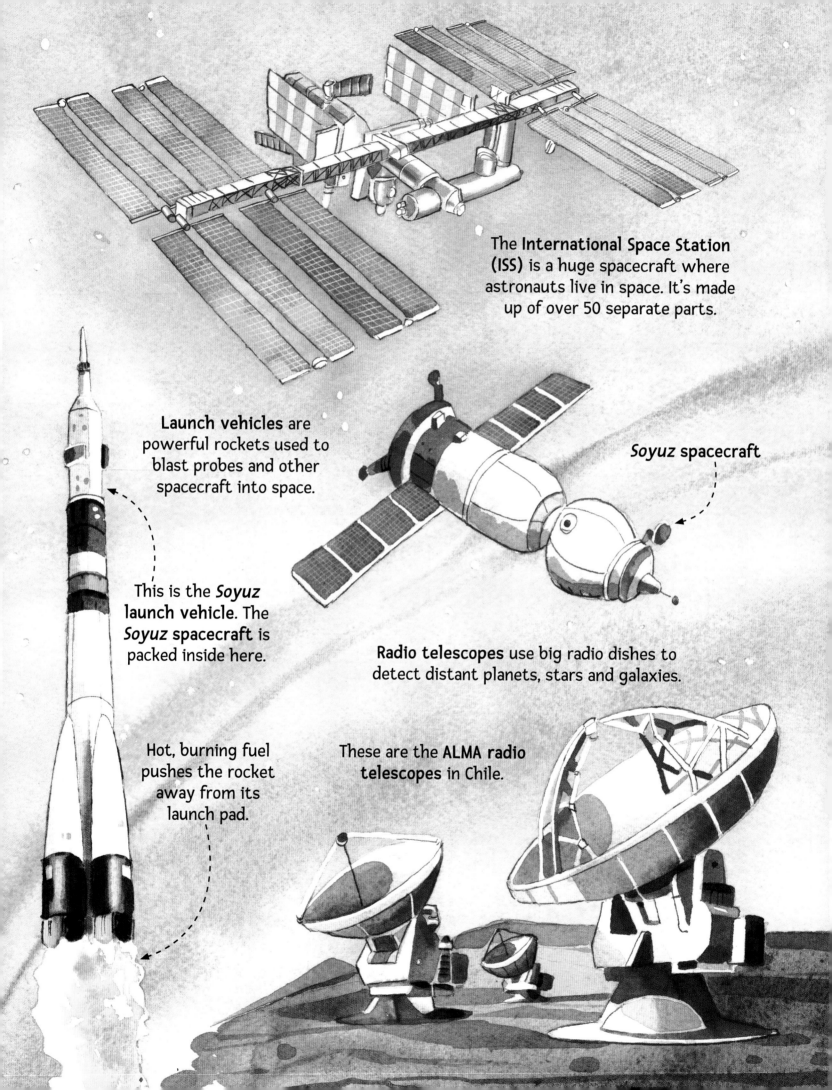

The **International Space Station (ISS)** is a huge spacecraft where astronauts live in space. It's made up of over 50 separate parts.

Launch vehicles are powerful rockets used to blast probes and other spacecraft into space.

Soyuz spacecraft

This is the *Soyuz* launch vehicle. The *Soyuz* spacecraft is packed inside here.

Radio telescopes use big radio dishes to detect distant planets, stars and galaxies.

Hot, burning fuel pushes the rocket away from its launch pad.

These are the **ALMA radio telescopes** in Chile.